Redeeming YOUR LOST BLESSINGS

Turning God's Blessings From a Mere Desire to a daily Reality

DENNIS KARANJA WAITIKI

Unless otherwise indicated, all scriptures are from the New International Version.

Redeeming Your Lost Blessings

2nd Edition
Print 2019

ISBN: 978-9914-9675-2-4

Dennis Karanja
Email: krnjdennis@gmail.com
P.O Box 70007-00400
Nairobi, Kenya
Tel; +254722 636 303

PUBLISHED BY:
Eword Publishers
Victoria Towers, Upperhill Nairobi.
PO Box 70007 - 00400
Tel: 0745 420 420
ewordpublishers@gmail.com

Table of Contents

Appreciation

Let me take this opportunity to sincerely thank my wife, Esther Muthoni Karanja. Her support during the writing of this book cannot be fully quantified. Because you believed in my vision to become an author, I too can now redeem my eternal blessing. May God empower you to be everything that He desired of you.

I also want to thank my two lovely daughters Juniper Wanja and Mehitabel Murugi. You may be young now to understand this, but when you do grow - for you will, know that you made it all worthwhile. The pride of being your dad and the desire to empower your destinies has been the engine for what I do.

I am also immensely grateful to my parents John Karanja Wilson and Karen Wanja Karanja. You have been the best role models I could have ever asked for in a parent. Your emotional, spiritual, and financial support cannot be overstated. Thank you.

Special thanks also go to my brothers Chris, Collins, Billy, and Eugene. You have thrown all care to the wind in the quest to help me succeed. I can never repay all your kindness; from the bottom of my heart, thank you.

And to the team that helped make the writing and launch of this book a reality, the organizing committee, the book launch team, my cousins, my family, my friends, and generally, the Body of Christ. May God see your generosity and sacrifice. And to my spiritual parents, Apostle John Kimani William and Reverend Naomi Kimani, I am eternally grateful for your guidance and support. Thank you

Dedication

I dedicate this book to everyone who desires to discover and fulfill their God given destiny. The value of live is discovered when you realize the reason you are here. This book is a tool to help you discover where you may have lost track of your eternal blessing - which is your true purpose in life.

Preface

This book contains two key sections. The first section is titled the ***2 Principle Deviations*** and the second is the ***7 Universal Barriers*** to your destiny. They are both the result of a season of prayer that I took to try and understand certain key questions about life; what I have seen in my own life and the lives of other people.

I don't know how many of the people you know personally, friends and family, are living **truly fulfilling lives**. And by fulfilling I don't just mean financially, but it's a good place to start. So let's start there; how many of the people in the family you come from, including yourself, are in the top 30 careers in this country. There are many more, but that's also a good place to begin. Are there any in your family who are either;

- Cabinet ministers, governors, senators, members of parliament or even the president.
- Company founders, directors, chief executives, financial analysts or top managers.
- Engineers; Nuclear, Aerospace, Chemical, Electrical, Biomedical, or Material engineers.
- Computing; software & web developers, IT, security, or game specialists.
- Doctors: neurosurgeons, anesthesiologist, and dermatologists.
- Pastors, bishops, apostles, prophets, or international evangelists.
- Pilots or cabin crews.

- Judges or lawyers?

But beyond that, how many of your friends and family, including yourself, are in truly happy marriages; have happy families with great loving children; or are in great relations with their in-laws. If there are some, how many, and if not why?

This is the query that this book seeks to unravel, and the answers are not what you might expect. During my research for this book, I learnt many remarkable lessons. One of the troubling ones is the fact that millions of people live and die poor and unhappy for a simple reason – **their lives are defined by fate.** They never get to realize just how extensively the paths their lives took became **pre-determined** earlier on in life against God's will. Yet, they never had the power to change it. They settled on the assumption that poverty and unhappiness is their lot in life.

There is an 85% chance that you are who you are right now because you are bound by ***Seven Universal Barriers*** mainly based on where and how you were born and brought up. The aim of this book is to illuminate these barriers, show you exactly how they affect humanity, and how to re-discover God's **initial blueprint** for your life. It marks a step by step path through which you can **redeem God's divine blessing** regardless of the limitations that have previously kept you from living your best life now. And you know what I have learnt through this experience is that poverty and unhappiness is in no way, shape, or form the will of God.

So whether you have ***deviated*** or ***been barred*** from attaining your destiny, it's not the end of life. You are among the living, which means there is hope for you. And this is, I believe, is a message from the Lord to help you redeem all that you have lost.

Dennis Karanja Waitiki

Introduction

For most people, life is more confusing than it is sensible. At any given point in life, we all find ourselves at a place where we wish someone would sit next to us and answer all the impossible questions that we regularly have. Why for example,

would you have a great educational background and yet live a miserable life?

Why would you be so beautiful or handsome but remain the unmarried one among your peers? Why would you have a great marriage but still be poor? Why would you have so much money but be completely desperate for true love? How can one work so hard and yet make so little income?

The whys are endless and the answers we have seem to be totally inadequate. To illustrate this aspect a little better, allow me to relate the stories of three prominent individuals that you may know.

Steve Jobs

On October 5th 2011, the world lost a man that is to date considered a legend in the field of technology; Steve Jobs. He was the founder and longtime CEO of Apple Inc., the maker of the wildly popular iPhones and Mac Computers.

And this title is by no means a small thing. By 2018, Apple Inc. was the world's largest technology company by revenue and one of the world's most valuable brands.

Yet, despite this kind of success, Steve still died of cancer. This man was by any measure of the word a genius. He was exceptional as a creative director, a manager, and a marketer. Today, having an Apple phone or a Mac is considered somewhat stylish. In fact, those who own Apple phones are the only ones who are not very keen on changing the default ringing tone of their gadgets. So why was such a brilliant and wealthy man unable to do anything about the pancreatic cancer he suffered from?

Marilyn Monroe

Anyone who has followed showbiz and celebrity lifestyles for some time has definitely come across this iconic figure. Monroe is still considered an icon of beauty and style for more than a century now. Born in June 1st 1926, this lady had a life that was far from perfect for most of her childhood. She was for the most part brought up by well-wishers since her parents divorced early in her life and her mother was mentally ill for much of her adulthood.

The tough upbringing forced her into early marriage that consequently led her into a modelling and acting career. Her life from then on was a mixture of fortune and tragedy. As a woman who did not shy away from showing off her stunning beauty, she quickly gained prominence as an actor. She appeared in various popular magazines, movies, and music albums. Her fortunes rose quickly as her fame grew.

Unfortunately for her, she invited trouble into her life in equal measure.

By the age of 35, Monroe had been married 3 times. She had gone through two miscarriages and had been involved in several affairs. She also struggled with alcoholism during this period. She died at the age of 36 years due to a drug overdose. To date, she is still considered the most celebrated beauty icon of all time. This young woman died at the prime of her life because of personal struggles and addictions despite her runaway beauty.

Billy Graham

This man is probably the most notable evangelistic icon of the 20th century. Born on 7th November 1918, Billy ran one of the most illustrious evangelical careers that span a period of 40 years. Rev Billy never had it easy starting off either, quite similar to the previous two individuals. And his rise to prominence took a long time.

However, during his lifetime, it is reported that Billy Graham personally preached to 210 million people in 185 countries through his worldwide missions. It is also reported that he led more 3.2 million people to accept Christ through his ministry. A fair estimate of his total reach through international crusades and broadcast media is thought to be about **2.2 billion people**. He was also a close spiritual adviser to 11 American presidents.

Upon his death on 21st February 2018, he became the first religious leader and the **4th private citizen** to be taken to the US capitol in Washington DC.

This is an honor that is only conferred to the most distinguished citizens in the US.

These three stories feature three prominent people who influenced humanity in different but profound ways. They were all endowed with amazing talents or gifts that defined their paths in life. Sadly, though, we still lost these unique men and woman despite all that they had to offer to humanity. Why did we have to lose Steve Jobs, an IT icon who died at an age that could still be considered young. Monroe's death was such a tragedy for a person who was at the prime of her life. Billy Graham truly touched the world, but we still lost this legend.

However, the differences in the nature of their lives, length of their days, and how they died tells a much deeper and more profound story. It portrays an oscillation between one who dies out of desperation, another out of limitation, and still another out of exhaustion due to old age.

Monroe had so much more to give, but she suffered desperation and died as a result of living a hollow and empty life. Steve Jobs was great, but he lost the battle due to the limited capacity of his body to deal with sickness. By the age of 99 years, Billy Graham's energy reserves were already fully exhausted and his physical body gave in to death.

For the most part, humanity falls somewhere in between **these three states** at the time of their departure from this world. It is this **basic framework** that forms the basis of this book and the many powerful lessons that we can all learn.

The Preacher

Solomon is probably the person in the Bible who best summarizes life from an objective point of view. In writing the book of Ecclesiastes, he was not trying to bring his readers closer to God. Instead, he was offering **his perspective as a person nearing the end of his life**. It's a philosophical introspection on life. But there is a more important reason why his words should matter to everyone.

In today's money, King Solomon's wealth is thought to have been about $2.2 trillion adjusted for inflation. This is according to various economists and historians. This makes him the 5th richest man in all of recorded history. This be-littles the wealth of other highly notable figures such as Mansa Musa of Mali at $415 billion, John D. Rockefeller at $367 billion, Andrew Carnegie at $337 billion, Henry Ford at $200 billion plus, and Bill Gates, the man best known to us today at $144 billion.

In fact, King Solomon was so rich that during his lifetime, silver was regarded as **common stone** in Jerusalem. It was a low value resource in the country. The Bible says that nothing in his household was made of silver. Each year, for the 39 years he remained King, he received 666 talents of Gold from other parts of the world. This translates to about **25 tons of gold per year**.

This goes to say, that Solomon had the capacity to try every pleasure thinkable to man – he had the ability to get anything from any part of the world from his fleet of trading ships. That explains why he married 700 wives of royal birth and kept 300 concubines.

Simply put, it is possible no one living today, anywhere in the world, will ever be as rich or as wise as Solomon was.

So what does life offer to such a man? What did he have to say about his exploits at the end of his life? He was a king, a global ruler, the 5th wealthiest man of all time, and to cup it all, the wisest man who has ever lived to date.

Below is a short excerpt from his preaching, which is really more of a personal dialogue.

I, the Preacher, was king over Israel in Jerusalem. And I set my heart to seek and search out by wisdom concerning all that is done under heaven; this burdensome task God has given to the sons of man, by which they may be exercised. I have seen all the works that are done under the sun; and indeed, all is vanity and grasping for the wind. What is crooked cannot be made straight, and what is lacking cannot be numbered.

I communed with my heart, saying, "Look, I have attained greatness, and have gained more wisdom than all who were before me in Jerusalem. My heart has understood great wisdom and knowledge." And I set my heart to know wisdom and to know madness and folly. I perceived that this also is grasping for the wind. For in much wisdom is much grief, and he who increases knowledge increases sorrow. ***(Ecclesiastes 1:12-18).***

The Vanity of Pleasure

I said in my heart, "Come now, I will test you with mirth; Therefore, enjoy pleasure"; but surely, this also was vanity. I said of laughter — "Madness!"; and of mirth, "What does it accomplish?" I searched in my heart how to gratify my flesh with wine, while guiding my heart with wisdom, and how to lay hold on folly, till I might see what was good for the sons of men to do under heaven all the days of their lives.

I made my works great, I built myself houses, and planted myself vineyards. I made myself gardens and orchards, and I planted all kinds of fruit trees in them. I made myself water pools from which to water the growing trees of the grove. I acquired male and female servants, and had servants born in my house.

Yes, I had greater possessions of herds and flocks than all who were in Jerusalem before me. I also gathered for myself silver and gold and the special treasures of kings and of the provinces. I acquired male and female singers, the delights of the sons of men, and musical instruments of all kinds. So I became great and excelled more than all who were before me in Jerusalem. Also my wisdom remained with me.

Whatever my eyes desired I did not keep from them. I did not withhold my heart from any pleasure, for my heart rejoiced in all my labor; And this was my reward from all my labor. Then I looked on all the works that my hands had done and on the labor in which I had toiled. And indeed all was vanity and grasping for the wind. There was no profit under the sun.
(Ecclesiastes 2:1-11).

VANITY – That's the one word that a man who had it all in life uses to describe his overall experience in life. That is a truly sad summary and grave future prospect for those who are looking for things.

It is quite common, for most of us, to think that we will be happier when we get things; a better car, a bigger house, marriage to a beautiful wife or well to do husband, better education, an extra degree, more money, more friends, more land, better shoes, more expensive clothes, and so on. According to the richest and wisest man in world history, all these do not equate to a happy life.

And, we don't have to argue about it. It is something all men eventually figure out by the end of their lives.

So, what really is the secret to a happy, blessed life? What is the purpose of living if it all ends up in un-fulfillment, desperation, and sadness? Must all men see life as vanity, a chasing after the wind? What really is the essence of life? Are we all prone to the dictates of fate? Do we have the capacity to take control of our lives and dictate how we are to live?

This is the question that this book seeks to unravel, to the extent that God has graced me. This book does not claim to offer all the answers or give a complete analysis to life. However, I will offer what I believe is an important eye opener to anyone who seeks to live a happy and fulfilling life. This is information that I gathered in my own quest to understand life from an objective point of view, as a believer in Christ Jesus, and as a human being. I can promise you that the book is a journey that is truly worth taking. May God give you understanding.

Part 1

The Principle Deviations

There are two principle deviations that have kept men from attaining definitive success in both physical and spiritual standards.

What does this mean?

Before we unveil the ***Universal Barriers*** to your destiny, you need to appreciate whether you are in the right path to begin with. You may have heard the expression, *as you climb the ladder of life, be sure its leaning against the right building.* Many people have lost the race of life because they took what was supposed to be a tool and made it their ultimate goal. This is what am calling ***a deviation*** and there are two of them as per the scope of this book. These are;

a) Talents
b) Blessings

Chapter 1

The First Principle Deviation – The Crash of Talents & Destinies

Quick Definition of Terms

Talent – is a natural endowment that gives an individual the ***special ability to do certain things***. Any person, from whatever faith, religion, race, gender, or educational background can have a talent. It is the natural ability to do something with ease that others may find hard. In most cases, people are driven to pursue certain courses and careers by either one or several of the talents that they have. For the purposes of this book, the terms talent and gift may be used interchangeably.

Destiny – This is a set of occurrences that happens in a person's life and especially those that are expected to take place in the future. The term destiny is used when one is ***able to control what happens to that future***. When one has no control however, the ***term fate is used instead***.

These two are basic definitions that most people are aware of. It is how the two affect our lives that makes all the difference.

In simple terms, talents **are tools** that God gives to all humanity to make us **better equipped for life**. Without these special talents that we find all over the world, the world would be a very different place all together.

It is because of these talents that we have all sorts of great and amazing things in this world. They have helped create great industries such as aviation, education, manufacturing, medicine, entertainment, art, construction, engineering, technology, and so many others. These natural abilities help men to constantly learn, create, and innovate. That is also why the world is such different place compared to the one that God initially created. And this is a good thing.

More importantly, ***a talent is a tool for the attainment of one's destiny***. Regardless of our descent or believes in life, we all appreciate the fact that we each have a unique purpose in this life. This is a fact that the Bible makes very clear. Every human being, male or female, ***is no accident to God***. We know that because it is what God told Jeremiah.

Before I formed you in the womb I knew you, before you were born I set you apart; I appointed you as a prophet to the nations." **(Jeremiah 1:5).**

Since God appoints us way before we are born, He also equips us with the abilities we now call talents. This makes you to sort of have a special power to achieve your lot in life; something that is not common to other people.

For example, if God appoints you to be a ruler, he may equip you with talents such as oratory skills, management skills, and leadership skills.

Elon Mask

Today, Elon Mask is widely known and highly regarded as an innovator. He is the founder of companies like SpaceX, Tesla, SolarCity, and The Boring Company. All these companies are based on very revolutionary ideas. I have consistently heard interviewers ask Mask one question - ***"How do you do it?"***

The reason why they ask him this question is that he is probably just one of two people to start and successfully run more than one billion-dollar companies. Most successful people do only one at a time. The answer he gives every time perfectly depicts how powerful a talent can be.

At one time he said that he first made a rocket as a young boy. He never knew that he would one day make one in real life – that is creativity. On another occasion, he said that he grew up a highly driven person. He knew he was somehow different from other young boys his age. It means he is a visionary.

In yet another interview, he said that he seems to see things in a way that other people don't; something that also surprises him. So what do we call that? I will leave that for you to answer. As you ponder that question, consider this;

With **SpaceX**, Ellon Mask is currently designing a rocket that will take man to Mars by about 2022. And this is not just a vague prediction. His company is currently the first organization ...

worldwide, governments included, to make re-usable rockets – rockets that can fly into space and land back on earth without getting damaged or crashing into the sea. In fact, the American government through NASA has contracted SpaceX with the task of taking supplies to the International Space Station (ISS) for a contract of $1 billion. Of these, Musk, through his company has already delivered these supplies 12 times.

His exploits with the three other companies; **Tesla**, **Solar City**, and the **Boring Company** are also amazingly innovative. I encourage you to read about them. The point here is, this is a man whose talent is changing the world literally. While this seems fascinating to us, God knew it before he was born and equipped him with matching talents. But that is not the whole story.

Why Is Humanity Still Broken?

Humanity, as innovative and advanced as we are today, is still broken because ***a talent is like an un-calibrated compass***; Its only when we surrender it to God that He re-calibrates it and places us correctly on the map to our destiny. The difference with a normal compass is that you have to go to the shop to buy one. However, in the case of a talent 'Compass' they come **pre-installed** within us. Just that they are not calibrated properly.

Working with such a gadget can be tough; we can try to set it ourselves and at times it may work to some extent. We may use it and go on great expeditions, through exciting places, but in the wrong direction.

At times, we may miss important junctions where we were meant to connect with our destiny helpers. We may also miss key stops where were are expected to pick additional tools for the journey.

There are also those who think that their compasses are useless, that they can't work. So they drop them and use their own human instinct. They may still succeed in life, but not to the extent that God would have wanted them to.

There are also those who get pre-occupied with the beauty and magnificence of their compasses. They spend their whole lives polishing and beautifying the compasses and forget the journey. People see what they have and marvel, forgetting that it was only meant to be **a tool not a destination**. This is what I call the **crash of talents and destinies**.

As important as talents may be, they only compose a section of the whole story. They are tools or resources that we have been given to achieve a bigger goal in life –destiny. However, when we make talents the goal, we deviate from our main focus. Sadly, the number of people who have done this in their lives is extensive. In fact, talents have become the main drivers in the lives of a majority of people living today all over the world. Not sure how that works?

Here is an example.

Francis Rono is a high school student at Kipkatech High school in Kapsabet. He is an average but disciplined student. Teachers love him because although he does not achieve grades that are high as the best student in his class, he is an inspiration to many.

He went on to win the same race during the IAAF World Under-20 Championships in Boston, US, giving Kenya one of the 10 gold medals the country won that year. Based on a pledge made by the Kenyan government 2 years ago, Rono bagged a minimum of Ksh 1 million as a reward for representing the country. This is besides other fees he could make in future such as appearance fees for record holders and special bonuses. The point is, he is talented and his talent has already made him a millionaire.

For most people, that is all that matters. They therefore focus on sharpening the talent – which is perfectly in order, and use it to make as much money as possible during their active careers life. The question is though, **is that all life is about?** Is that all that Rono can achieve with his life as a talented athlete? We would't know - Its only when he goes to God for the calibration of his compass – the talent, that he can then be certain about his destiny. And here are some examples from the Bible.

Ephesians 2:10

For we are God's handiwork, created in Christ Jesus to do good works, which God prepared in advance for us to do.

***James* 1:17**

Every good and perfect gift is from above, coming down from the Father of the heavenly lights, who does not change like shifting shadows.

We are God's creation and everything we have was created for a purpose, **nothing is accidental.**

When we don't appreciate this fact, the extent of our success falls short and our achievements become limited. For Rono, and each one of us, there is more to life. **Here is a story** that will help you understand this principle more clearly.

Breaking 2

On Sep 21, 2017, National Geographic Studios released a very inspirational documentary on a project by Nike dubed ***Breaking 2*** – you should check it out on YouTube. This was an attempt by Nike as a company and three elite athletes to break the **2-hour barrier** for the world marathon race. The athletes were Eliud Kipchoge from Kenya, Lelisa Desisa from Ethiopia, and Zersenay Tadese. The three of them are highly accomplished athletes holding major world titles.

A bit of a background – Running for under 2 hours for the standard 26 miles of the world marathon has been a long standing debate and an almost impossible feat. The world marathon first became a standard race in 1921. That was also the first time that a man ran the race in **under 3 hours**. Since then, almost 800 races take place every year around the world.

By 1991, the world's best time for the marathon stood at **2:06:50.** That is 1 hour, 6 minutes and 50 seconds. Today, the world record for the same race stands at 2:02:57 held by **Eliud Kipchoge**. This was the fastest a man had ever run in a marathon. However, scientists always thought it was theoretically possible to complete the race in 1:57:58 in perfect conditions.

The Breaking 2 project by Nike was an attempt to offer the best possible conditions, scientifically and technologically to achieve this. Eliud Kipchoge won the race with a personal best time of 2:00:25, thereby breaking his own previous world record. This was only 25 seconds shy of running below 2 hours.

His performance in this race made him the first human to run that fast, and many around the world now consider him somewhat super-human. The most inspirational part of Breaking 2 for me is not the record, but the determination of one man, driven by destiny to impact humanity. You see, Eliud Kipchoge is as mentioned the fastest Marathon runner in the world today; he is rich by any world standard, and now quite famous. But that did not stop him from pursuing more than just money and fame.

Through Breaking 2, Eliud has become a legend, his name will be mentioned for many years to come. He will also be the basis of numerous scientific studies for athletes, sports shoe makers, and numerous interest groups. He successfully avoided the deviation of focusing on his talent and chose to pursue a bigger call in life. That is the essence of not crushing your destiny at the feet of your talent – and instead, using your talent as a compass on the road to your destiny.

Today, Eliud is not only an inspiration in the field of athletics, but he now offers talks in major organizations and top learning institutions around the world. You can be rich and that's fine; you can be famous and that's also okay; but I would rather you leave this world better than you found it. Its greater and better than fame and money.

Chapter 2

Second Principle Deviation - Pursuit of The Wrong Blessing

So, how many types of blessings do you know. Think about it. I will wait….

Did you know that there is a certain type of blessing you ought not to pursue? In fact, pursuing this type blessing goes against the word of God. Yet, this is exactly what probably 70% of us do today. This is what the Bible says about the blessing I am referring you to;

"Therefore, I tell you, do not worry about your life, what you will eat or drink; or about your body, what you will wear. Is not life more than food, and the body more than clothes? Look at the birds of the air; they do not sow or reap or store away in barns, and yet your heavenly Father feeds them. Are you not much more valuable than they? Can any one of you by worrying add a single hour to your life?

"And why do you worry about clothes? See how the flowers of the field grow. They do not labor or spin. Yet I tell you that not even Solomon in all his splendor was dressed like one of these. If that is how God clothes the grass of the field, which is here today and tomorrow is thrown into the fire, will he not much more clothe you—you of little faith? So do not worry, saying, 'What shall we eat?' or 'What shall we drink?' or 'What shall we wear?' For the pagans run after all these things, and your heavenly Father knows that you need them. But seek first his kingdom and his righteousness, and all these things will be given to you as well. Therefore, do not worry about tomorrow, for tomorrow will worry about itself. Each day has enough trouble of its own." ***Matthew 6:25-34***

You may probably already know this scripture by heart, but you may never have heard it in the way am about to present it to you today. But first, here are two categories of blessings we shall look into in this book.

a) The Manna Blessings
b) The Eternal Blessing

The Manna Blessings

First an introduction. The journey of the Israelites in exodus chapter 16 is arguably the greatest journey ever taken by the human race. It was a journey that was initiated by God for the sole purpose of taking the Israelites from the hands of the Egyptians and away from a life of slavery.

The promise was to take them to a land filled with milk and honey. The idea was to give them a happy prosperous life full of blessings and fellowship with God. The problem that was that it was a journey and through the desert; no doubt very tough. It was also probably the part that the Israelites never truly understood to begin with. So, after almost 2 months of being in a desert and experiencing the hardships of the journey, they started to grumble. They complained that the real aim of Moses and Aaron was to bring them out into the desert to kill them there.

Moses, being a faithful servant, went to God and presented their complaints to Him. And since God clearly had a plan from the beginning, He promptly sent them manna and quail. In fact, the Bible says they had bread and meat (manna and quail) for the next 40 years. This happened on a daily basis without fail except on the Sabbath days.

However, God was not happy about the approach that the Israelites used to address their challenges. By complaining, they seemed to insinuate that He was unfaithful. It purported that God never had a plan when he brought them out of Egypt and into the desert. In fact, by accusing Moses and Aaron of planning to kill them, they were accusing God of planning to destroy them.

Now imagine the same scenario, but in this case we have children accusing their father of bringing them into this world with the sole aim of killing them. That would mean that the father never had a plan of taking care of the children he intentionally bore.

My feeling is that no father can be amused by this. In fact, this could quickly bring an end to a relationship between a father and Child. Yet, this is exactly what happened between God and the Israelites. By appearing to care about themselves more than God possibly would, they were purporting to have a better idea about life than God did.

In hindsight, this looks very foolish. Yet, it is exactly what most people do on a daily basis. The Bible tells us to make our requests known to God and to believe that He will fulfill every prayer and petition that we make. When we don't do this, we abandon the innocent surrender of a child to a father and actually try to parent ourselves.

This is the exact message that Jesus Christ was passing in ***Matthew 6 chapter 25***. The point is, when God allowed you to be born into this world, he knew exactly what you needed even before you first figured it out. Now, by abandoning God and turning your life into a persistent and daily pursuit of things shows a lack of faith in God.

And this is why I call these types of blessings ***manna blessings.*** They are kind of blessings that God is obligated as a father to provide to you anyway. That is why God provides rain, sunshine security, safety from diseases, accidents, keeps our children safe, and wakes us up every morning after a deep night sleep. ***Manna blessings are not our responsibility***; they are God's obligation. So, when you put God aside and purely focus on seeking daily provisions, you are literally going against the word of God. Manna blessings are to be received by a simple petition to God in faith.

The Eternal Blessing

Eternal blessings are what we generally call **destiny or purpose** in life – as defined in the previous section. It is also what we can refer to as the **reason for life**. This is what every human being is innately created to pursue.

I am yet to meet a single human being who desires to live a life without meaning. Every person wants to feel that their life had meaning here on earth. Even the people who live in the toughest parts of the world do have aspirations of become someone great in life, even when that means taking serious risks. And that's exactly what God desires of us.

Going back to the story of the Israelites, the key to fulfilling their journey to the promised land highly depended on focusing on the main goal. The goal was not to focus on the food they would eat on the way, or the people they would meet, or how much fun they would have on the way. It was paramount that all of the Israelites understood this when they set out on this journey. Failure to focus on this key goal meant losing sight of life itself. Yet, that was exactly what they did.

On numerous occasions, the Israelites went against God on a quest to meet their own daily needs and desires. While it may have seemed quite clear what they were to pursue when they left Egypt, they seemed to suffer from a regular loss of focus ever so often. Unfortunately for them, and for so many others in our day, ***loss of focus on your purpose is a loss of focus on life itself.***

When life lacks purpose, the chances that it may cease to exist stand tall. That is why animals can die any day and it's not such a big deal. It seems quite normal since the life of a single animal doesn't cause any major alarm. It is purpose that defines the value of life. It is the pursuit of destiny that gives life meaning. This is what God envisioned when He created each human being.

This goes a long way to explain what we are seeing on the news today almost on a daily basis. Scores of people are being swindled into giving away their money to unscrupulous 'Preachers' simply because they have their priorities set wrong. You see, the pursuit of destiny is not an event, rather, it is a journey. Whenever you set out on a long-term journey, you are not fixated on what happens here or now. Your plans, goals, and your desires are tied around that which you seek to attain at a later date.

It is this kind mindset that sustains life until such a time when that goal is achieved. You are able to bypass discouragement, criticism, short failure, or abandonment. You convince yourself that, despite the seeming short term troubles, there is greater good to come in future.

That's why the Bible says ***where there is no vision, the people perish.*** If your goal is to achieve success in an instant, then you become prey to those who peddle fake miracles. When your focus is on instant achievements, then you live a life that is focused on instant gratification with short term benefits.

And this is something that the devil has truly used to his advantage. He has learnt the art of shifting priorities ***– which I call a principle deviation***. By creating the illusion of falling into sudden destruction, he is able to build up desperation and offer an easy escape. Unfortunately, when you fall prey to his scheme, you do so on your own. You are left to pursue manna blessings on your own without God's guidance. You see, God cannot empower you to waste valuable resources in pursuit of what he has already provided. It's like sending an army to a war that has already been worn.

And because the devil understands these dynamics, despair offers him a golden opportunity for him to ***deviate you***. You basically surrender the control center of your life to an enemy bent on ruining you. You may right now be crying and asking God why he has forsaken you. You may be wondering why your life is not blessed. You may even be feeling as though you live under a curse. Yet, what really happened is that you lost focus on what is truly important. You have fixated your attention on running after what you already have.

So, what should you do if you find yourself in this position? Two things.

First, understand the word of God. Stop worrying and do the right thing;

"Do not be anxious about anything, but in every situation, by prayer and petition, with thanksgiving, present your requests to God." ***Philippians 4:6-7***

It's that simple, letting God know what you need and moving on. Don't waste precious time praying for days on end for manna. God understands what you need and he will provide. The only reason he may not is when you are walking in rebellion or in doubt. That can easily eliminate God's capacity to act in your life or on your behalf.

Secondly, refocus your life. And that is not a complicated thing to say. It simply means understanding what you ought to be in life and exerting more energy, including prayers towards achieving it.

What I have noted is that it is very easy to get consumed with the daily troubles of life. Issues such as 'how do I get to work in time, 'how do I avoid traffic', 'how do I get rent this month', 'how do I cater for school fees', 'how should I deal with the needs of my parents'... all these can be very overwhelming. These issues can even include serving in church. You may be an usher, a praise team leader, an intercessor, and so on, but still be disconnected with your true purpose. When this happens, you need to step back, and re-look at your life, then decide which trajectory will lead you to your true destiny.

Does serving in the security department prepare you to be who you truly desire to become. Is the time you are spending in the intercessory team making you better in terms of your true purpose in life? If not, you could easily be wasting precious time right now. This is where you take time off and seek God diligently to understand what your true purpose is and which route will take you there quickest. Are you even serving in the right church?

You may be so fixated in a ministry in Kenya and totally lose sight of an organization God is hoping you would start sooner in an Asian country, for that's your true calling.

The beauty about our God is that He answers prayers, and especially those that have the bigger picture in mind. Consider these verses.

Jeremiah 23:23 *Am I only a God nearby," declares the Lord, "and not a God far away? Who can hide in secret places so that I cannot see them?" declares the Lord. "Do not I fill heaven and earth?" declares the Lord. There is no situation you may possibly have that God does not know about.*

James 4:3 *You ask and do not receive, because you ask with wrong motives, so that you may spend it on your pleasures.*

Most people wrongly believe that you cannot trust God with simple needs. You might be thinking that he might not answer you based on how and when you need it. He does provide, but he gives what is fitting and useful. When you focus on the eternal blessings, God gladly takes up your manna needs.

And two more for your consideration;

Isaiah 59:2 *But your iniquities have made a separation between you and your God, And your sins have hidden His face from you so that He does not hear.*

John 9:31 *"We know that God does not hear sinners; but if anyone is God-fearing and does His will, He hears him.*

The first and important phase of redeeming your lost blessing – your destiny in life, is knowing how to avoid these to principle deviations. When you do, thenyour ladder is definitely 'leaning on the right building'. The second phase, which is what we are getting into, is understanding ***the Universal Barriers to Destiny.***

Part 2

The 7 Universal Barriers to Destiny

What are these barriers all about and what is their relationship to redeeming your lost blessings? Let me put it this way; destiny or your purpose in life is the eternal blessing that God expects you to pursue.

When you rightly pursue your destiny, you get a complete package of both purpose and provision. That is, you attain your purpose in life and all the additional blessings that comes with that purpose.

It's something similar to getting a scholarship. Students who show brilliance easily get scholarships because they offer great value to society or their sponsors – they are therefore provided for in all their needs during their educational life.

Those who are not as brilliant have no one to sponsor them. When you show a deep hunger for the pursuit of your destiny, heaven sponsors that desire by providing for your daily needs – manna blessings.

When you don't you lose both the eternal blessings and the manna blessings that come with it.

The aim of this book is to help you restore both of these blessings – thus Redeeming Your Lost Blessings.

However, until you understand

Part 1 – **Avoiding the principle deviation and**
Part 2 – **Overcoming the universal barriers to your destiny**, you may not fully redeem your lost blessings.

So, this second part of the books is aimed at helping you understand what these ten barriers are and how to overcome them? They are:

- Mental Barriers
- Cultural Barriers
- Regional Barriers
- Parental Barriers
- Ancestral Barriers
- Spiritual Barriers
- Marital
- Barriers

Chapter 3

Mental Barriers

Mental Incapacitation

A few years back, a friend of mine invited me to join a business networking forum, in Westlands, Nairobi, Kenya. Since it was on short notice and we had to be there very early, I didn't pay much attention to my dressing since, well, I was used to attending meetings. I later wished I had. I became conscious of the type of meeting we were going into the moment we arrived at the venue – The Azure Hotel. It is a high end establishment and way above my level at the time

My esteem dipped a little as my mind thought of all the possibilities in terms of who I would meet and what they might expect me to say. But my friend kept assuring me that he knew these people and we would be fine. May be I would just say a word or two, but nothing to worry about, really.

But, when we got off the lift and into the meeting room, I lost all confidence in myself as a human being. There definitely had to be people who were much more endowed in life than I already knew. Besides their unique mode of dressing, their skin color looked like money – if you know what I mean. The kind of skin color that tells you, *'please understand that I am rich'*.

All that I could do at the time was reach into my pocket for a handkerchief to wipe off fear from my face. But that made it even worse - I noticed a tear on my side pocket that I had not seen before. I almost screamed! Of all the calamities that would happen in the world, why did it have to be a gaping hole on the side of my pocket.

I tapped on my friend's shoulder and bid him goodbye. I could not stay there any longer. I was woefully unfit for the occasion. But before he could he could say anything, a very friendly, wealthy looking lady approached us with a broad smile on her face. Then she said, "Oh so sorry, hasn't anyone welcomed you yet? Please follow me!" I knew that the hope of ever redeeming my image was gone forever.

I walked slowly behind my friend, like a lamb headed for slaughter. She ushered us to a seat with two other ladies and a gentleman. Then she walked away, but not before feeding me to the lions. "We have a new guest", she said to them. "Please make him feel welcome." I sat there frozen like a Dasani water bottle in a freezer.

I gave simple yes or no answers to them as they went to great lengths to make feel welcome. This went on for some time until the question I most dreaded was served to me on a 'plate'. The 'plate' meaning I could not ignore it; I had to say something tangible, and think it through before I did. It was one of the worst party-moments of my life.

"Eeeh…! Oh me? You are asking what I do? I aaah…, I started off trying to gauge exactly which one of my skills that far carried the most weight. "I am a copywriter!"

Just so you know, I was still doing writing at the time, but I had only read about copywriting in passing. So, I knew a little about what it was. I thought it was complicated enough for anyone trying to figure out what I do.

"Copy writer? What is a copy writer? It had worked. They did not know what that was and I gladly took the opportunity to explain. I combined the little knowledge I had on the subject and my background as a writer to offer the most convincing answer possible. So, I told them how, 'we as a company' created business related content for local and international companies with the aim of helping them attract more customers and thus more business.

The 'we as a company' I was referring to only existed in my mind at the time. But that did not stop all those to whom I explained my business model to marvel. They confessed that they had never thought that writers and entrepreneurs could work together in that way. In essence I applied a business idea I had only toyed with in my mind to a 'hostile business environment' and it worked. In fact, I left the meeting with a torn trouser and two business deals worth Ksh 25,000.

I only had one regret though - if only I had been more confident, I would have done better. Had I not allowed my mind to incapacitate me so severely, I probably would have talked to more people and netted more deals. I registered Eword Publishers soon after and it still runs to date. One of the jobs I did for a client from that meeting would later help him seek a grant worth $7 million from a Middle East investor.

A Limited Mental State

That is what I call ***mental barriers***. It is a mental state that limits your capacity, despite your skills or educational background, to achieve. When faced with unfamiliar situation or experiences that we are not used to, the barriers become even more pronounced.

Sometimes, we get so used to having these barriers that we don't even notice that they are affecting us. We learn to operate with them and they naturally become part of us. That is why some people will not even dare walk into certain hotels; but when they do, they squeeze themselves to one side of their seats as though they are sorry for being there. And when the menu arrives, they will either just look at the drinks column or scan the entire thing for the lowest possible
price.

I remember the first time I got invited to a Java Coffee joint and it makes me laugh at myself. When I arrived at the joint, I stood a few feet from the entrance and would only occasionally peep inside to see if I could spot my host. When I finally got in, I tip-toed to where he was seated keeping my eyes glued to the floor lest I offended anyone.

Even when we started talking, I kept my voice low. It was as though someone would have heard me talking and asked, "*We unaongea nini na mara yako ya kwanza hapa?* (What is it that you are saying and it's your first time here?)

My friend had to constantly remind me that it was okay to be loud since it was a public space.

I am sure this is something we can all relate to. There is always that thing in life that feels out of reach to you as an individual. There will be moments in life when people or places will make you feel intimidated or inadequate. It is how you deal with your mind in that situation that makes all the difference.

You see, mental barriers are the exact opposite of faith. They are a tricky balance between faith, foolishness, and rationale. The Bible puts it this way;

And without faith it is impossible to please God, because anyone who comes to him must believe that he exists and that he rewards those who earnestly seek him. (Heb 11:6)

Think about Peter, the disciple of Jesus for a moment. We are told of the story where Jesus and his disciples had gone out to preach and it was on that occasion that He fed five thousand people. After the open air meeting, Jesus asked his disciples to go out ahead of him into the boat. He stayed behind to dismiss the crowd and soon after went out to the mountain to pray.

At the fourth watch of the night, which is at about 3am in the morning, he went out to them into the sea walking on water. When the disciples saw him, they were terrified and thought that he was a ghost. Note here that you cannot have fear and faith at the same time; one will have to push out the other.

Now, take note – the Bible says at that moment, the disciples "were terrified. "*It's a ghost*," *they said, and cried out in fear*". (Matt 14:26)

But immediately Jesus spoke to them asking them not to be afraid, Peter spoke out and said, *"Lord, if it's you," Peter replied, "tell me to come to you on the water."* Is that not amazing?

Think about it; this was the first time ever that Peter had seen someone walking on water. But the simple conviction that Jesus gave him at a moment of fear and terror was all he needed to dare out into the unknown. This section of the Bible is often quoted in reference to Peter's lack of faith. But I think this was a great portrayal of one who had a bold and daring spirit. And that earned him a place among the heroes who have ever walked on water in world history.

For most people, mental barriers are the one thing that keeps them from achieving the very best in their life. It is the thing in their mind that keeps telling
them;

- You can't
- You are not good enough
- You are not one of them
- You don't belong there.
- It is too hard for you
- You might die if you try.
- No one in your family has ever done it.
- What will people say if you fail.
- It's safer to stay here with everyone else.
- What if they judge me harshly or laugh at me?

Here are some factors that you should always bear in mind whenever mental barriers try to keep you from daring out.

a) People are more attracted to success than they are to people who are trying out new things. That is why we know about all the great innovators who made it and nothing about those who tried and failed. Many laughed at the prospect of the then Senator Obama becoming president until he actually did. That was when the whole world stopped being skeptical and celebrated him.

b) Everyone's destiny is unique and different. So, if the only things you try out are what everyone else is doing, you may never fulfill your purpose in life. Facebook CEO, Mark Zuckerberg will tell you this. They have written most of the technology driving Facebook today; majority of that information did not exist in any textbook before they created it. That is why social media technology is not yet a major subject in mainstream IT schools.

c) What you are capable of achieving is way beyond your mental comprehension right now. In most cases, you only discover what you are capable of when you venture out into the unknown. And that how the world keeps advancing. What we see today did not exist a century ago, and most of it will be faced out a century from now. What will be your contribution to this world during your lifetime?

One last story as I close this section.

Israel

In 2017, I had the privilege of visiting the land of Israel on a tour of the Holy Land. Besides being spiritually transformational, it also challenged my way of thinking on many levels. For your information, Israel is currently rated as one the 15 most technologically advanced nations in the world. Their technology in agriculture, water recycling and conservation, as well as the making of silicon chips is phenomenon. It was fascinating to experience some of these advancements in real life.

However, this was also the first time I used another currency other than our local Kenyan Shillings. However, that presented a major challenge to how I regarded money. So, there would be these instances where we would walk into a shop or restaurant in need of something. The first thing was of course asking how much the price of an item was. In other cases, the prices would be indicated in the price tags.

Although I had the money, my mind would almost always try to calculate how much that same item would be valued in Kenyan shillings. For example, there was this snack that they called falatel. It's sort of a deep fried bread made of chickpea that is often taken with salads. Most food joints sold it at between $8 and $10. Covert that to Kenyan shillings and that's about Ksh 800 to Ksh 1,000.

At first I would flatly refuse to pay that much for a piece of bread. How could I buy a piece of bread for a thousand bob when you get an even bigger piece back at home of a mere fifty bob. Well I did that until one the men we were travelling with jostled me to reality.

He said,
"Dennis, you will die here if you keep walking around with a Kenyan mindset. You are in Israel now, so drop it."

And I did. You see, bread may have even be free back in Kenya, but the truth was, if I wanted to live, I had to buy food at the Israeli rate.

Let me use that example to say this, unless you drop the knowledge of what is common to you and dare out, what you will achieve in life is very minimal. Drop that mindset and dare to dream. This is key ***in redeeming your lost blessings.***

Chapter 4

Cultural Barriers

By a show of hands, how many of you come from a culture that has deep set traditions and customs that you are still expected to follow regardless of your education or faith? Okay, I see.

That is what this section is about. Since this may challenge how you view things, I only ask that you allow me to indulge you for just for a moment. You can still do things the way you are used to, but just hear me out and consider what I am about to say.

Our Source

First off, when God determines that a new child should be born into this world, only He understands who the child will become. Although we now have technology that can show us a child's gender, weight, and a few other things, most of everything else is a mystery. The personality, skin color, tastes, likes and dislikes are all unknown even to the parents, let alone the rest of us.

But since a child cannot grow up on its own, God has to identify a set of two people who can come together and bear this child.

Where anyone is born is purely God's choice; and that could be anywhere in the world. A parent can pray for a boy but end up with a girl or vice versa. Someone may even desperately desire a child but never get one. It's purely God's choice.

This, therefore, means that a child is born with a clean slate. It is unaware of its gender, language, race, culture, or nationality. That child can grow up anywhere and become anyone. A newborn child can learn any language and belong to any culture, depending on whose hands God allows it into.

It would therefore make more sense to know who we are as individuals by referring to God's original intention rather than the intentions of those we are born to. This is what I mean; how do you determine your purpose in life? Who do you ask? What do you use to define who you are as a person? That seems obvious but it's not.

It is fascinating to me how, the One who first knew you and actually determined how and where you would be born – that is God, ends having little or no say on who you become in life. The people who seem to have the greatest say are your immediate family, relatives, and the society around you. And to understand just how twisted this can be, read this verse again.

"Before I formed you in the womb I knew you, before you were born I set you apart; I appointed you as a prophet to the nations." ***(Jeremiah 1:5)***

What God was saying to Jeremiah here is that He did not wait for his mother to conceive him to say, "Oh that's Jeremiah?" No.

God knew Jeremiah even before his mother determined that she would have a child. That's how far back God's knowledge about us goes.

But what happens when we are born? In some cultures, we are told that a child has to be taken to his or her grandmother for some acceptance rituals. They start owning you up and defining the course of your life right from birth. In some places, the father and mother are visited by family members for an induction into how ***'we as the so and so tribe/family/clan do our things'.*** Some cultures go as far as saying that they do not accept a certain child because he or she does not meet their standards.

Think about it; what contribution does anyone have on your existence here on earth? You may argue that they gave you life. That they are the reason that you are alive. But let me ask you, is God not the reason we are all alive?

I am a father of two lovely daughters, and so I am not being unreasonable to parents. What I can tell is that up until the time each one of them was born, I felt so helpless on whether they would live or die. I often had questions like would they be healthy? What will their personalities be like? Will they be normal children or unique in some way? Will they be able to walk or talk in good time?

If you are a parent, you know what I mean. In all the 9 months before birth and after, we just sit there and watch. Tell me, what can you do to change what God has already determined. For a new born, for example, you can't even tell whether they are sick or healthy.

They just breast-feed and you can only hope that the milk is doing 'something' in them to make them grow up.

Yet, all the culture custodians later have the audacity to come and say, ***for you to belong, this is what you must do***. ***For you to be a real man, or woman, you must follow this ritual or live by this custom.*** I dare say, we belong because God wills it, not because someone thinks it. What you need to be alive, **right now is life – the one that only God gives**. You don't need anyone's rules, or to be bound by culture to be alive. And I say this with all due respect to our elders.

If any cultural rule goes against the world of God, would it make not make more sense to respect God and not men? I mean, God can strike down a whole nation and help a fatherless child to grow up in the same breath. Have you not heard that of children who are thrown away after birth, and yet they still grew up to become great people?

Steve Jobs, the man I told you about in chapter 1, the late CEO of Apple Inc. was given away for adoption before he was even born. Did that stop him from forming one of the most innovative companies in the world? No.

And don't get me wrong here. I am not condemning every custom out there. In most tribes or families, certain customs are put in place to help people live right. They are installed to help people live within certain boundaries of morality. The customs that I am referring to in this section are those that go against the will of God. It is those customs that ascribe more to a demonic foundation rather than the worship of God.

Here are two examples.

The Day of the Dead – Mexico

This is a public holiday celebrated in November 2nd every year in Mexico and other Latin American countries. This is a day when people remember their departed one and do certain rituals in their honor. For example, in some places, people paint their faces like skulls and walk around the streets at night with candles. They also visit the graves of their loved ones where they take flowers, the clothes they used to wear and even the food and drinks that they loved. There is a general belief that the departed ones awaken from their eternal sleep on this day and join them in the celebrations.

They also make Ofrendas – small personal alters made at home in honor of the dead person. Popular symbols during this celebration is skeletons and skulls. The symbols are used in making candies, cakes, masks, and dolls. They are also adorned in various apparel. And before you think this is just something done by a few people, it's a major national celebration in Latin American countries. What do you think? Is it a nice culture?

Baby Jumping – Spain

The people who hold this custom in Spain believe that the best way to keep infants safe from the devil is to jump over them. Yes. But in this case, a man dressed like the devil and jump over infants who are laid on mattresses in the streets. This is an old tradition dating back to 1620.

According to them, this ritual cleanses their original sin. And don't even think that this is a small event. It is often so big that whole towns will gather as parents bring in their young ones to partake the ritual.

This pagan tradition was and still is so strongly entrenched in the country. In fact, when Christianity came into the country, they had to compromise and allow it to continue. Do you know of any traditions back at home that the church has had to allow to exist alongside the Christian faith?

I know these are extreme examples, but I believe they get the message across perfectly.

Why Does This Matter?

Let me pose this question to you once again; how do you determine your purpose in life? Who do you ask? What do you use to define who you are as a person? In addition to that let me ask you, to what extent has the customs and traditions you found back at home defined who you are today?

Culture is such a powerful barrier to destiny considering that its God who initially determines our purpose in life. If, for example, a 'devil' has to jump over your child for her to have a shot in life, does God still have any say in that life. What rituals did your parents have to take you through after you were born? Do you think such activities are currently keeping you from achieving your best in life?

I can tell you for sure, unless you reject and denounce some of these traditions, they may forever influence your life and those of your children after you. Rejecting some of these customs is a major step in redeeming your lost blessings. The Bible says in **Deuteronomy 5:9**

Thou shalt not bow down thyself unto them, nor serve them: for I the LORD thy God am a jealous God, visiting the iniquity of the fathers upon the children unto the third and fourth generation of them that hate me.

As I had said before, the blessing that God provides for 100% is the **eternal blessing**. When you pursue a path beaten out by the wishes of others, you live on **manna blessings** all your life. Your life becomes a constant pursuit of things. However, God is willing to set anyone free who may have been locked down from progress by this and other barriers. I believe it is the reason He allowed you to get this book and read it. S***top pleasing people and pursue your destiny***.

Chapter 5

Parental Barriers

This barrier is largely intertwined with the previous section. It basically looks at how parenthood is such a powerful determinant of who we become in life. This is because parents are the initial contact that anyone has with the world. Parents are also a child's mentors and teachers for 20 to 30 years of life. They are major destiny connectors when they follow God's plan for your life.

The Power of Parenthood

What this means is that parents can either promote a person into a life of blessing or one that is wrought with struggles. Millions of people around the world today can directly attribute their success or failure to their parents. There are hundreds of factors that a parent defines early on in one's childhood. This can include;

- Where you live
- When you school
- The friends you make early on in life
- Your career path

- Your character and personality
- Likes and dislikes
- Where you end up working and so many other factors.

There are scores of people I know that are in certain careers today because their parents made the choices for them. They pursued certain courses because that's what their parents wanted them to. Yet that is not what they truly wanted to become. They have therefore abandoned their true passions and are instead fulfilling their parent's agenda.

While we cannot choose the parents we are born to, it is critical that you understand the extent to which your parents have shifted or supported your purpose in life. God may not have found you the perfect parents, but he did give you the ability to become what you needed to become. It is all in you.

Look at it this way, God does not give us a perfect world to become who we ought to be. What he does is provide all the tools you need within you. The problem is when you do not realize your environment, your parents included, may be influencing or affecting your rise to your destiny. God brings us to our parents with the understanding that they will instill within us a set of skills necessary for our destinies.

Parents are given a critical role by God to get you to a certain place that will help you step into the next level in life. For some people, parental obligation ends right after delivery. For others, it ends way beyond employment and marriage. The challenge is understanding their role and how far it spreads out into your life.

It may extend too far and limit what you can achieve. It may also end too soon and forever cripple your life. In either of these cases, a person is called upon to seek to understand their original Blue Print for this life. The role of the parent is critical, but it's not the only thing we need in life.

How far have your parents influenced you to into being who you are today? Have they made you better or worse of? These are critical questions that everyone should consider at any point in life. What you need to appreciate is the role they have or are still playing in your life and how that is affecting you today. If the effect is negative, then some things need to change right away. If their influence is positive, then you need to invest more in them.

Here are some facts to bear in mind;

a) Parents are destiny keepers – they custodians of your eternal blessings to a certain extent. You cannot ignore that. Your job is to determine how far. That's also why we need to give them their rightful respect and support either way.

b) When parents act as per the will of God they push as closer to our eternal blessing. When they don't, they can pull us away from it. This calls for wisdom is dealing with good and bad parenthood.

c) You cannot blame your parents forever. Parents have been given control of your life only to a certain extent, not completely.

Therefore, if you spend all your life blaming them, then you are wasting precious time and energy in the wrong place. Break free from whatever parental barrier that is keeping you from your destiny. Ask God for wisdom and direction on how to do this.

James 1:5 says, *If any of you lacks wisdom, you should ask God, who gives generously to all without finding fault,*
and it will be given to you.

d) Every parent is answerable to God on the custody they have on their children's destinies. Any parent who callously handles the destinies of their children will have to directly answer for it to God. Parenting is a job given to every parent by God. It is therefore expected to be executed according to his will. Don't be one among the parents who have ruined the destinies of their children or led them to an early grave.

b) Your destiny is ultimately yours. If a parental barrier has kept you from success in life, God is aware of it. Ask Him for help and He can show you the way around it. You don't have to give up or life the rest of your life in regret.

Ecclesiastes 9:4 says, *Anyone who is among the living has hope—even a live dog is better off than a dead lion! The fact that you are reading this means that you are among the living and there is hope for you.*

Jeff Bezos

On September 2018, Forbes Magazine named Jeff Bezos to be the richest man in the planet with an estimated personal wealth of $150 billion. This is largely attributed to the success of the now world famous retail giant Amazon. However, this journey to the top started 25 years ago. This was after he accepted $300,000 from his parents to start the company.

This money in essence became the seed that gave birth to a brand that is currently worth over $1 trillion in market capitalization. The secret to Jeff Bezos blessings today can be directly attributed to his parents. Had he rejected that help at the time. That would have become his greatest barrier in life.

The idea here is to understand how parental barriers affect us. And God does give us this understanding when we ask. We cannot do away with our parents, but understanding the role they play in your life maters to your overall identity in life.

The idea here is to understand how parental barriers affect us. And God does give us this understanding when we ask. We cannot do away with our parents, but understanding the role they play in your life maters to your overall identity in life.

Chapter 6

Ancestral Barriers

This is a barrier that this section of the book is woefully limited to fully handle. It is a wide topic that thousands of books cannot fully handle. But I will try to illustrate it as best as possible with a few stories. This subject is more thoroughly dealt with in the **2nd Edition** of this book.

The Nixon Clan

I listened to a story given by Pastor Derek Prince, a man who is deeply knowledgeable about the subject of curses and blessings. It is about a woman he prayed for to break a curse in her family that dated back **four centuries**. The woman was of Scottish descent and she came from a clan called Nixon. Through historical evidence she discovered that her family was currently living under a curse.

This was attributed to clan wars between the Scottish and the English in the **16th century**. As a result of the wars, history showed that the Bishop of the Church of Scotland at that time had put a curse on her clan. No one could have thought much about it except for the fact that what the bishop had said would happen was still taking place in that clan four centuries later.

It was this discovery that led her to Pastor Prince to be prayed for, thereby breaking the curse. ***Ancestral barriers are largely attributed to curses and blessings*** that follow families many generations after the one who brought them are gone.

Unfortunately, most people live and die in suffering without ever discovering what was affecting them. They basically become slaves of fate. They live a life that they don't seem to understand or have control over.

Unless someone understands the problems and addresses it directly, they may forever be bound in life. This understanding helped me to understand just how important it is to **pray against generational curses**. This is when one goes before God ***in prayer and fasting, genuinely seeking for God's revelation on this matter.***

There can be many outcomes to such prayers. For example, God can lead to you to a member of your family who may have knowledge what could be ailing you. This can help you pray and repent on behalf of your ancestors in a deeper way and with clear knowledge of the issues. God can also answer you through revelation. This can give you a clear understanding of what to pray for.

God can also help you to abandon certain plans, or projects or to separate with certain people who have connections to ancestral curses. This is one of the toughest barriers to deal with, but also critical for anyone who wants to redeem their lost blessings.

The Curse of Jericho

We are told of the story in the Old Testament where Joshua issued a curse on the city of Jericho after its defeat. At that time Joshua pronounced this solemn oath saying;

"Cursed before the Lord is the one who undertakes to rebuild this city, Jericho: "At the cost of his firstborn son he will lay its foundations; at the cost of his youngest he will set up its gates." Joshua 6:26.

This curse was fulfilled in the book of **1 Kings 16:34**, which was **500 years** after Joshua issued the curse.

This is what the Bible says,

In Ahab's time, Hiel of Bethel rebuilt Jericho. He laid its foundations at the cost of his firstborn son Abiram, and he set up its gates at the cost of his youngest son Segub, in accordance with the word of the Lord spoken by Joshua son of Nun.

I don't think the effect of a curse can be more explicit than that. Imagine words spoken by one man taking effect after five centuries.

Let me put it to you that your life right now could be in the mess it is in due to words that were spoken against your ancestors hundreds of years before you were born. And throwing your hands up in the air and saying, "So what can I do?" doesn't change that.

What does make a difference is an earnest prayer made to God for deliverance. I believe God brought these things to my attention because he hungers for people who are purpose driven.

However, He does see just how far these barriers are keeping his people from discovering the calls in their lives.

You may be stuck in poverty, a broken marriage, failed businesses, inability to grow in career, inability to proceed with education and so on.

And all these could be the function of a curse that was brought down from your ancestors. You may not have known but God does. And He is asking you now to genuinely seek Him for help.

Here are three ways you can overcome ancestral barriers;

i. Confession of Sins - 1 John 1:9 - If we confess our sins, he is faithful and just to forgive us [our] sins, and to cleanse us from all unrighteousness.

James 5:16 - Therefore confess your sins to each other and pray for each other so that you may be healed. The prayer of a righteous person is powerful and effective.

ii. Separating yourself from the sin and unrighteous of your ancestors -

Deuteronomy 5:9 - *Thou shalt not bow down thyself unto them, nor serve them: for I the LORD thy God [am] a jealous God, visiting the iniquity of the fathers upon the children unto the third and fourth generation of them that hate me.*

Ezekiel 18:19 - *"Yet you ask, 'Why does the son not share the guilt of his father?' Since the son has done what is just and right and has been careful to keep all my decrees, he will surely live.*

iii. Receiving Christ into Your Life -

2 Corinthians 5:17 - *Therefore if any man be in Christ, he is a new creature: old things are passed away; behold, all things are become new.*

Chapter 7

Religious Barriers

The People's Temple – Jonestown

This is a purportedly Christian establishment that came to light worldwide in 1978 after 909 people, 304 of them children committed suicide. However, this was just the end result of activities that had been going on for years. The People's Temple was a church established by Jim Jones, an ordained minister in 1956 in Indianapolis, US. Besides the preaching of the word of God, it was involved in numerous humanitarian activities, including racial integration and anti-racial discrimination protests. This endeared him to the media, politicians and church in general.

The church was affiliated to the Full Gospel church before and more autonomous organization. Jones vision was to create a movement where there was no separation between races and everyone was equal before God. Later though, questions started arising about allegations of harassment and inhumane treatment of the church members.

In 1977, Jones convinced a few hundred of his members to move to Jonestown. Jonestown was a settlement that Jones had built for several years in Guyana, a country in South America. This move was to allegedly aimed at creating a sanctuary that was serene and away from interference from external interference. It would be a socialist paradise to freely worship as they pleased.

Investigations into the religion however started showing strange activities within the camp. Jones is said to have tested the members' loyalty to him by giving them juice lazed with poison and asked them to drink it. This was done often although it was just a test.

However, when the American government started intense investigations, things turned tragic. An American congressman named Ryan was shot dead by members of the sect while leaving Jonestown on an investigative trip. Knowing that the government would get involved, Jones gave instructions for all his followers in the camp to take juice that had cyanide poison, which they did. Children were also made to drink the poison by their parents. In total, 909 people died that day. That is the power of faith, and in this case, faith in the wrong thing.

The Thin Boundary Line

Let me put it this way, there is a very thin line between faith and foolishness. No faith in this world, regardless of what it promises, should take away the power to think for yourself. No religious leader has been given the power by God to demand unquestioning loyalty to them.

It saddens me so deeply when I see the number of people who have totally lost direction in life courtesy of a certain religious establishments. The purpose of faith should be to promote our well-being here on earth and beyond. When a given spiritual leader then claims that you should totally neglect yourself and follow or serve them, it should raise serious questions.

I know this is a very touchy subject that whips up emotions among many people of faith. Nevertheless, that should not keep us from addressing these issues critically. Millions of people, especially in poor nations, have totally lost sight of their own destinies. They have done this while all the while helping a few select individual live in utter opulence and luxury. In fact, many people who are dealing with hardships in life have fallen prey to these 'wolves in sheep skin'.

Religion is a major barrier to so many destinies. Sadly, many people have dedicated their lives to cults masquerading as churches and houses of worship. These establishments brain wash them and take away any hope of ever realizing who they would have been in life. They are fed with teaching that are based on personal convictions rather than the Word of God.

It's so unfortunate when someone lives their whole life poor and distraught just because they made sacrifices for a purported 'Man of god'. Children born to such people are even worse off because they don't really have the freedom of choice at a young age. How does someone convince you to abandon education, your job, your family, and give up your money, yet they themselves are living large?

How to Identify a Cult

I read an article in the Atlantic that I think beautifully summarizes how one can identify a cult. So allow me to share it here.

- Opposing critical thinking
- Isolating members and penalizing them for leaving
- Emphasizing special doctrines that are outside of scripture
- Seeking inappropriate loyalty to their leaders
- Dishonoring the family unit
- Crossing Biblical boundaries of behavior (versus sexual purity and personal ownership)
- Separation from the Church.

If the faith you ascribe to matches any of these traits, you need to take a step back and relook at your beliefs. Take time away from your 'church' and take an objective look at what you are involved in. Involvement in a cult can utterly ruin the fabric of your life. No one man should replace God in your life. If your faith is largely based on pleasing a religious leader and seeking their approval, then there is a problem.

In fact, many good Christians are living cultic lives in perfectly good churches. They have objectified their pastors and bishops to an extent that they are now gods in their lives. They often use phrases like, "The Man of God said" in the place of "the word of God says."

In the places of worship where this is rampant, men and women who were initially driven by the desire to serve God turn around and become gods to their followers. They become manipulative, conniving, irreverent to God. Their church business from then on become a major self-enrichment project. I know you can relate to this because of the numerous dramatic incidences we have seen in African nations in the recent past. Kenya has also sadly fallen prey of such religions camouflaged as genuine places of worship.

May God give you understanding so that you do not surrender your precious blessings to a worthless cause. Our God is very jealous when he sees the millions of people whose destinies are getting ruined daily. His desire is to see you becoming what he intended you to be in the first place.

I Have a Theory

I believe that if your reason for attending any church or place of worship is to find God and serve him, you are safe. Even if you accidentally get involved with the wrong religion, He will help you identify and flee from it.

However, when your goal shifts to other things, you are at risk. This could be either the desire to get rich, gain popularity, or catch the attention of the 'man of God'. God examines the motive of everyone's heart and helps them accordingly. If your desire is not God, why should He get involved. You will get coned, lied to and manipulated because you are on your own. Desire God and he will help you redeem any blessing you have lost to religious barriers.

Chapter 8

Marital Barriers

Solomon's Foreign Wives

The book of 1 Kings 11 tells of a story of how King Solomon lost his Kingdom, cutting short his God given purpose because he loved many wives. This is the Biblical account;

King Solomon, however, loved many foreign women besides Pharaoh's daughter—Moabites, Ammonites, Edomites, Sidonians and Hittites. They were from nations about which the Lord had told the Israelites, "You must not intermarry with them, because they will surely turn your hearts after their gods." Nevertheless, Solomon held fast to them in love. He had seven hundred wives of royal birth and three hundred concubines, and his wives led him astray.

As Solomon grew old, his wives turned his heart after other gods, and his heart was not fully devoted to the Lord his God, as the heart of David his father had been. He followed Ashtoreth the goddess of the Sidonians, and Molek the detestable god of the Ammonites. So Solomon did evil in the eyes of the Lord; he did not follow the Lord completely, as David his father had done.

On a hill east of Jerusalem, Solomon built a high place for Chemosh the detestable god of Moab, and for Molek the detestable god of the Ammonites. He did the same for all his foreign wives, who burned incense and offered sacrifices to their gods.

The Lord became angry with Solomon because his heart had turned away from the Lord, the God of Israel, who had appeared to him twice. Although he had forbidden Solomon to follow other gods, Solomon did not keep the Lord's command. So the Lord said to Solomon, "Since this is your attitude and you have not kept my covenant and my decrees, which I commanded you, I will most certainly tear the kingdom away from you and give it to one of your subordinates.

King Solomon had it all. He had more than most people in world history will ever dream of. As indicated in the first chapter of this book, he is one of just a handful of the richest people who ever lived to date. Unfortunately, the one thing that took it all away was marriage. He seemed to have a very twisted idea of marriage. Marrying a thousand wives is far from normal.

Fortunately, in our day, very few people marry more than one wife. However, that does not negate the fact that marriage can be a powerful barrier to destiny. This is ironical because marriage partners are also some of the most critical partners to our destinies. A marriage partner always...always defines the path to your destiny.

God had given very clear instructions to the Israelites not to intermarry with the heathen. He understood the extent to which a partner in marriage can alter the intent of the heart.

For Solomon, that intent became building alters for the gods of his wives. In the quest to please them, he turned away from God and thereby lost what King David had worked so hard to attain.

The Balancing Act

The Bible says that when two people get married, they become one. Its therefore not logical to say that you can live in God's will and successfully remain one with someone who hates the matters of God. In time, one will alter the intents of the other. And this is critical since pursuing your destiny is a life long journey; and so is marriage.

It's not easy to get this point across to someone who is not yet married. The extent to which a marriage partner impacts your marriage is not very apparent at that stage. Before marriage, love, attraction, beauty, and good looks seem to carry more weight. After marriage though, other matters take center stage. These may include faith, finance, family, and relationship.

Unfortunately, it is before marriage that one needs to make critical decisions that will affect the rest of their lives. Marriage to a partner not in the will of God almost automatically spells doom to your destiny. Trying to balance the pursuit of your purpose in life and pleasing your partner is impossible. The only way that both of this things can work together is when you marry someone who appreciates and empowers you to pursue your call in life. Marriage to someone in the will of enables to strike that balance.

Before marriage, there is an opportunity to make the right decision. And God is eve ready to help on this matter, because he understands its gravity. That's why Proverbs 19:14 says,

Houses and wealth are inherited from parents, but a prudent wife is from the Lord. It's totally God's business to connect you to the right partner.

But what if you never involved God in marrying your current partner? The answer to that question is not simple or straightforward. I therefore cannot purport to have all the answers here. What I know though is that it's a gamble; your partner can buy into your vision or ignore it. In most cases, you are forced to take a compromised path. It's not exactly what God would have wanted, but you are also not so badly off. For you to fully discover and fulfil your purpose, you have to work harder for both you and your husband or wife.

Paul puts it this way in 1 Corinthians 7:12–16,

To the rest I say this (I, not the Lord): If any brother has a wife who is not a believer and she is willing to live with him, he must not divorce her. And if a woman has a husband who is not a believer and he is willing to live with her, she must not divorce him. For the unbelieving husband has been sanctified through his wife, and the unbelieving wife has been sanctified through her believing husband. Otherwise your children would be unclean, but as it is, they are holy. But if the unbeliever leaves, let it be so.

The brother or the sister is not bound in such circumstances; God has called us to live in peace. How do you know, wife, whether you will save your husband? Or, how do you know, husband, whether you will save your wife?

It is through faith in Christ that we can redeem our eternal blessing. If one partner does not believe in this God, then the other partner should work hard and pray for them to come to Christ's saving grace. If they refuse and choose to live, then according to Paul, let them leave. Anything in between is a compromise.

Chapter 9

Geographical Barriers

Does God Know Where You Live?

You know I often wonder, who would I be if I didn't live where I do right now? Would I be better off or worse of? Really, think about it. How much has your current locality determined who you are as a person. I know we have often said jokingly about certain places, *"I definitely can't live there."* Or *"I hate that neighborhood"*.

However, there are **two key factors** I want to bring to your attention right now.

First – Yes, geographical and physical location largely determines who you become in life.
That explains why different people from different places have accents in their speech. You speak the language that you do today because of where you live right now. In fact, geographical location affects many more factors than we care to think about. These include;

- The people we live with and call our community The level of education you can attain – access to high or low quality education in various regions of the world.
- Your speech, language, articulation, and diction – for example, compare those who live up-country and those who are born in cities.
- Your level of exposure and knowledge – for example, access to the internet and information.
- Your economic well-being – life is often tough when you live in a poor country.

These are just a few examples. For instance, due to the long drawn wars in Syria and the Middle East, most residents have had to flee to other countries in search for safety. This has led to hunger, poor access to basic needs, little or no time for formal education and very poor economic well-being.

What was their fault? Why did they have to go through this? I don't have all the answers, but one thing am sure is that, being Syrian is one reason. The fact that they were physically there when the war broke out made them direct targets.

There are numerous opportunities that will by-pass you in life for the simple fact that you are Kenyan or African. Sad as that sounds, it is true. There are also people who may have been way better off in life had they been born in Kenya. There are certain traits that will stick with you for the rest of your life, just because you lived in the village for most of your childhood.

And who can we blame for that? Is it God? Is it your parents? Was it their parents before them?Will your children blame you in future for bringing them up in the place where you live right now? The answer is in ***factor number two.***

Secondly – God is interested in where you live.
Acts 17:26 says;

From one man he made all the nations, that they should inhabit the whole earth; and he marked out their appointed times in history and the boundaries of their lands.

Interesting as that sounds, it says a lot about the decision making process we go through when choosing where to live. If you never involve God when deciding where you should stay or work, let me tell you today – ***it's a grave mistake***. Here is why.

Time and Location Matters

The fact that you are alive right now, this minute, is because God decided that you should be. If you were born 100 years ago, all what is currently surrounding you would be a jungle or a thick forest. If you were to be born 200 years from now, the place you are standing or seated on right now would probably be in the middle of an expansive metropolis. You get the point. Time matters and God determines it accordingly.

On the other hand, if you were to relocate to Jamaica right now, how do you think your life would turn out in 5 years?

The reason you are where you are today is because God determined it that way before you were born. You may have found your parents in some remote village, but God may have determined that they should be there.

The reason I say ***may***, is because we are not always where God requires us to be. You may be in Kenya right now, but had you listened to God, you would be in another country. You see, due to the critical impact your physical location has on your overall life and what you can achieve, God is heavily invested in that. The purpose for which he called you **cannot be fulfilled anywhere or anytime**. God's assignments are for a **specific period and a specific time**.

Therefore, if you just woke up and moved to Jamaica today, your destiny could dramatically get altered or get totally abandoned. What this means is that you may be struggling in life because when God's angel of provision arrived in the town where He initially assigned, you were nowhere to be found. And since certain provisions are only useful in a certain location, they couldn't be brought over to where you are.

For example, if someone contracted you to build them a house, they would expect to find you on site when the materials arrived. Do you think you could still keep the job if your boss came to the site and missed you on three separate occasions? Definitely not. Unless the job is not important to him. The same principle applies with spiritual assignments – **location matters**.

So, find out from God where He expects to find you this year. That may sound funny, but I assure you, it's critical. There are blessings that you will only be able to redeem when you know your rightful geographical location for this particular season in life.

Epilogue

Redeem Your Blessings Today

Redeeming your lost blessings is really about understanding and dealing with all the factors that limit the ability to get **the eternal blessing.** This blessing **is your destiny**. It is the package that comes with everything else that you will require in life. This can be a happy marriage, a great carrier, and purpose driven life, great kids, and generally a happy, fulfilling life.

Many are living lives that a continual struggle in pursuit of manna blessings – ***things and provisions***. Yet, it is God's job to provide for those. That's how he feeds the birds of the air and the lilies of the valley. When we understand what we need to do, God fulfills what he must do.

Are you desperate, poor or unhappy? Find out whether you have deviated or been barred by any of the factors highlighted in this books.

As you can tell, the information contained in this book is not the kind that you can seat down and think of. You can come up with ideas of how to make your life better, but I believe God knows best. The only way to understand God's best is by asking him; telling him what you need.

The only way you will fully realize your blessings and overcome all these barriers is through surrender to God in prayer. Ask him to help you. He allowed me to share this with you because he loves and cares for you. I am only a messenger here to lead you to the one who sent me.

Speak to God right now and tell him to help you overcome any barrier that is keeping you from living your best life now. He says he is God both when you are near to Him of far away **(Jeremiah 23:23)**.

But most of all, give your life to him. Who is better at managing something than the one who initially made it. You are here because God wants you to. And it is his will that you live a fulfilled and happy life.

Shalom.

www.ingramcontent.com/pod-product-compliance
Lightning Source LLC
LaVergne TN
LVHW050336160826
845677LV00014B/3644

* 9 7 8 9 9 1 4 9 6 7 5 2 4 *